Trash Mountain

Ellen Catala

Contents

Rigby®

A Harcourt Achieve Imprint

www.Rigby.com
1-800-531-5015

From Trash to Treasure

There is a saying that "one person's trash is another person's treasure." This is certainly true of the Norman J. Levy Park and Preserve in Merrick, New York. As hard as it may be to believe, this beautiful park was once a landfill. In other words, it was once a very large pile of smelly trash!

My classmates and I visited the park recently. Luckily, my mom and dad got to come along, too. I'd like to share with you some of the things we learned and saw that day. I will always remember the experience, and maybe someday I can use what I learned to design more parks like this one.

This is me!

Before I begin, I want to say thank you to our guide Terrance. He was really nice and seemed to know everything there was to know about the park. We first met him at the amphitheater, which is the park's outdoor classroom. He told us a little about the park's history, and then showed us a map of where we would go on our tour.

Terrance greets visitors to the park in the amphitheater.

Many kids in the class had questions about the landfill that was right under our feet. Most of us had never thought much about trash before, except when our parents asked us to take out the garbage. So what did this park that we were visiting have to do with taking out the trash? Terrance explained it to us.

The bottom line is that the trash you throw out has to go somewhere. Think about how much trash your family throws out each week. Then think about all the families in your city throwing out their trash. That's a lot of trash!

What would we do without the trucks and the workers who take away our trash every day? Do you know where your trash goes?

After your trash leaves your home, it usually ends up in a landfill. The landfill is probably on the edge of town, away from homes and stores. No one wants the landfill nearby, but so far there is no way to just make it disappear! So, the trash is packed down, covered with dirt, and left to decompose, or break down into tiny bits that mix with the soil.

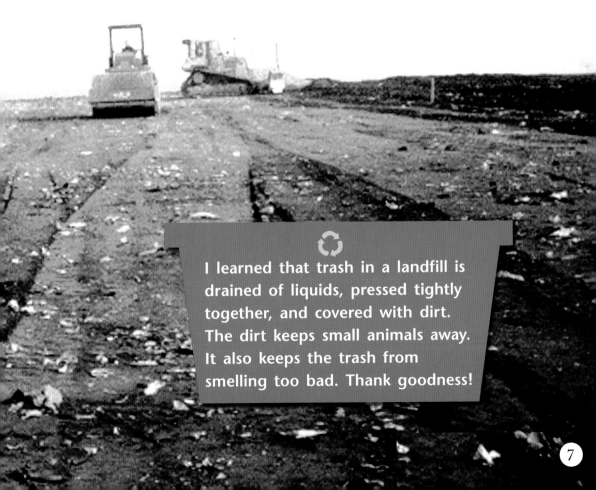

I learned that trash in a landfill is drained of liquids, pressed tightly together, and covered with dirt. The dirt keeps small animals away. It also keeps the trash from smelling too bad. Thank goodness!

Unfortunately, it takes a long time for trash to decompose, or break down, especially in a landfill where the trash is so tightly packed together. Some trash never decomposes, which is why it's important to recycle plastics and other materials that don't decompose easily.

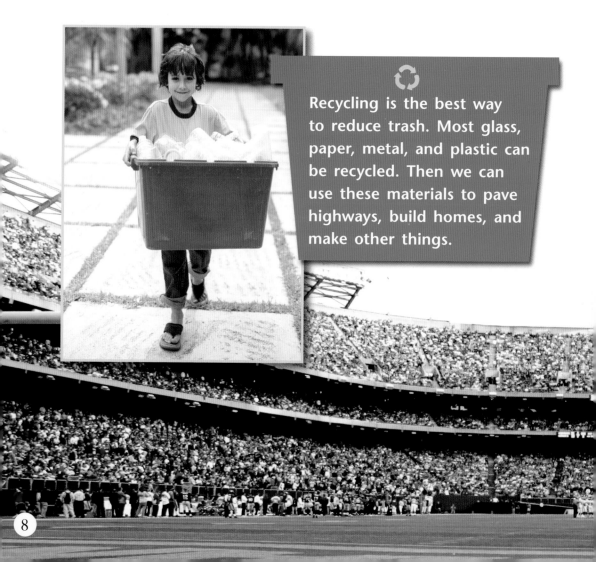

Recycling is the best way to reduce trash. Most glass, paper, metal, and plastic can be recycled. Then we can use these materials to pave highways, build homes, and make other things.

Once the landfill is full, nothing much can happen. Or can it? What if people were able to put a "cap" on the landfill and keep it covered? Could we then work and play on the top of that heap of trash?

The answer, surprisingly, is yes! That's exactly what was done at the Norman J. Levy Park and Preserve. It's also been done in other places with large landfills. Sixteen years after the landfill was full in Merrick, New York, it was covered and turned into a park. In other places, such as the Meadowlands in New Jersey, the landfill was covered, and sports and entertainment buildings were built on top of it.

I couldn't believe that this huge stadium in New Jersey was built on a landfill.

On Top of the Heap

The Merrick Landfill was open from 1950 to 1984. Most of what was dumped in it was ash from trash that had been burned. As each layer of ash was added to the landfill, a concrete ring was built around it. By the time the landfill was closed, the heap measured 50 acres across and 150 feet high!

Capping a landfill means you have to cover the trash with a very strong sheet of plastic. Then you have to cover the plastic with layers of dirt.

The trick to reusing a landfill for other purposes is proper capping, or covering with a strong sheet of plastic. Any dangerous materials in the landfill have to be protected so they don't harm the environment. No liquid should mix with the water supply, and nothing should ever leak out of the landfill. Vents, or holes, have to be put in to allow gases from the decomposing trash to escape from the ground.

What People Are Building on Former Landfills

- stores and parking lots
- sports stadiums
- airport runways
- tennis courts
- ski slopes

Plans for a Park

Once the Merrick Landfill was closed, it stopped being useful. The landfill was anything but dead, however. Many kinds of trees were growing out the sides of Merrick's trash mountain. Trash is very rich in nutrients, which are the parts of food that make plants and animals grow. As trash breaks down, the nutrients go into the soil and provide food for plants.

The Merrick Landfill took up valuable space. A plan was made to put that space to good use. That's what I want to do some day.

With the high price of land around New York City, it seemed a shame to waste this big, beautiful space. Plus, it wasn't good for the environment to leave the landfill uncovered.

Where is the Merrick Landfill?

New York

New York City

Long Island

Merrick Landfill

People who were experts in finding new uses for landfills were asked to draw up a plan to use the Merrick landfill in a creative way. First, they wanted to leave the tree-covered sides alone and just cap the top. Second, they wanted to turn the top into a park that was also a safe home for wildlife. And that's what they did!

Norman J. Levy Park and Preserve

- includes 52 total acres
- is 115 feet high at highest point
- opened October 22, 2000
- cost $15 million to build
- is home to 75 species of fish and crabs, and 35 species of wildflowers

New York City, with all of its tall buildings, is only 24 miles away from the Norman J. Levy Park and Preserve.

From the Norman J. Levy Park and Preserve, you can see for miles around. You can see beautiful Merrick Bay on the South Shore of Long Island outside New York City. You can see part of Jones Beach on the Atlantic coast. You can even catch a glimpse of the New York City skyline, which is one of my favorite views!

The Park and Preserve

Things to See and Do

The Norman J. Levy Park and Preserve offers many great sights and experiences. It includes two ponds, three miles of hiking trails, and a 500-foot-long fishing pier. The fishing pier is made of a wood from Peru called *Cumaru*. This wood is strong and doesn't splinter easily. Most importantly, it does not contain anything that might harm the environment.

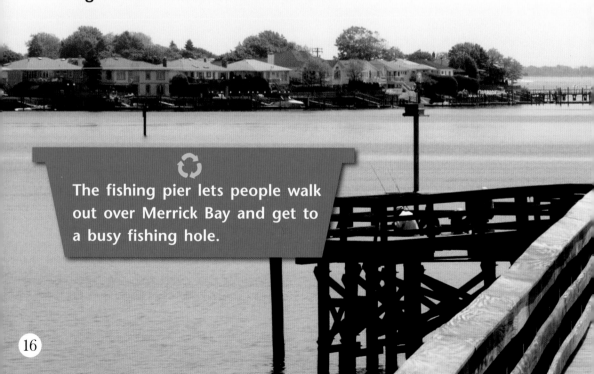

The fishing pier lets people walk out over Merrick Bay and get to a busy fishing hole.

The park also has a kayak and canoe launching ramp that enters a natural brook. The brook empties into Merrick Bay. While we were there, we watched some very skilled kayakers launch and paddle away. It made me wish I had a kayak!

My dad showed us how to use the ramp to launch a kayak.

On the Boardwalk

There is also a wooden sidewalk, called a boardwalk, beside some wetlands. Wetlands are areas where the land is covered in a few feet of water. Many different kinds of plants and animals live there.

Wetlands are important to people, too, because they help create fresh drinking water. The many plants in a wetland take harmful substances out of the water. Then the pure water seeps into wells.

The boardwalk lets people walk across the wetlands and see all the wildlife.

As we crossed the boardwalk, Terrance told us to look up. We saw a large bird just floating overhead. He told us it was an osprey. Osprey are hawks that like to make their nests on top of trees or tall poles near water. Their favorite prey is fish.

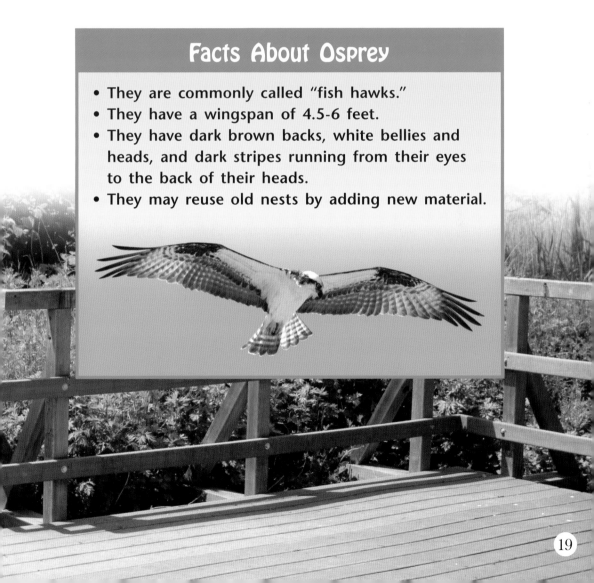

Facts About Osprey

- They are commonly called "fish hawks."
- They have a wingspan of 4.5-6 feet.
- They have dark brown backs, white bellies and heads, and dark stripes running from their eyes to the back of their heads.
- They may reuse old nests by adding new material.

Trail to the Top

After our walk on the boardwalk, we hiked the 3.3 miles of trails to the top of the park. Terrance pointed out the many different kinds of trees, bushes, and other plants. The air smelled so fresh, you'd never know you were hiking on a pile of trash!

From time to time, we stopped to try out exercise stations that were put in all along the trails. Each station stretches a different muscle group, giving you a good workout.

Signs at each excercise station show people how to use the station. My dad did 10 pull ups!

When we reached the high point in the park, Teresa asked us to tell her how many water towers, radio towers, and church steeples we could see. Would you believe we counted 20 water towers, 10 radio towers, and 7 church steeples? We also saw a lighthouse and a golf course.

This is the golf course we saw. It was so green! My dad said he wished he had some golf clubs.

Two Ponds and a Windmill

We stopped for lunch near one of the two ponds in the park. The ponds were made by people, but they look completely natural. Many ducks and geese were there to keep us company as we ate. Terrance told us the ponds have minnows and goldfish to keep the number of mosquitoes down. That's good, because I hate mosquito bites!

When this pond was dug, it was lined with a thick material. This is for extra safety to keep the water in the pond from mixing with any landfill below it.

One of the most interesting sights in the park is the windmill. It looks so nice when the breeze makes the blades turn. Terrance explained that the windmill runs a pump that makes a waterfall into the ponds. This keeps the water in the ponds moving so it stays fresh. The windmill even has a solar panel that runs a small light. The light is a warning to low flying planes not to hit the windmill!

This windmill can be seen for miles around. When people see it, they think of the park.

Birds, Butterflies, and More

As we walked around the park, we spotted dozens of different kinds of birds and butterflies. According to our guide, birdwatchers love the park and visit often. They come to see birds such as tree swallows, redwing blackbirds, great and snowy egrets, and black-crowned night herons.

The butterflies enjoy the many kinds of wildflowers growing in the park. As you look across the fields of flowers, you can see lots of butterflies flying around. They are so beautiful!

One interesting fact we learned is that the parking lot and trails were made with crushed seashells. This makes a good surface for walking and running. However, it's also a favorite surface of the turtles who live in the park. They like to lay their eggs right on the crushed shells, so we had to watch our step.

Turtles and tortoises often lay their eggs in places where people may walk, so you need to be careful.

For the last half hour of our visit, we went back to the amphitheater. This was our last chance for questions, and we all had a few. One of my friends asked how the park got its name. Our guide explained that it was named for a special man who worked hard to make this part of New York a better place. This man was New York State Senator Norman J. Levy.

This is the marker that tells the name of the park. It will help me remember this great place.

Senator Norman J. Levy, who lived in Merrick, New York, worked hard on laws to protect the environment and the rights of people with disabilities. When he died, people from all over the state wrote letters of sympathy to newspapers and to Senator Levy's family. Organizations such as the United Cerebral Palsy Association of Nassau County praised his work and said he would be greatly missed.

Because of Senator Levy, many things in the park support the environment. Capping the old landfill was a major step in improving the environment. The windmill also uses wind power to do work, rather than using electricity or gas. In addition, the park also has signs asking people to recycle.

Norman J. Levy worked hard to help people.

To support Senator Levy's work, the park also meets many needs of people with disabilities. There is a jitney, or a large golf cart, for those who cannot get around well on their own. Many parts of the park, including the fishing pier, have been built to be reachable even if you can't walk. The jitney can take you right to them because they were all built with ramps instead of steps.

I think Senator Norman J. Levy would be proud of this park named for him.

I asked lots of question about the park designers. The guide said that to do their kind of work you need to know math and science. But most of all, you need a creative mind. We all agreed that the people who planned this park were very creative!

This jitney helps park visitors that have disabilities.

An Amazing Place

The Norman J. Levy Park and Preserve is a great place to visit. It's also an amazing solution to a tough problem: what to do with a mountain of trash. To me, the park shows that even the things we throw away can be turned into something useful, and perhaps even beautiful. Obviously, I'm not alone. The park has more than 6,000 visitors every month. Maybe I'll see you there!